CONTEN

CW00543700

Poetry Book Society

CHOICE SELECTORS RECOMMENDATION SPECIAL COMMENDATION	MONA ARSHI & ANTHONY ANAXAGOROU
TRANSLATION SELECTOR	HARRY JOSEPHINE GILES
PAMPHLET SELECTORS	NINA MINGYA POWLES & ARJI MANUELPILLAI
CONTRIBUTORS	SOPHIE O'NEILL MEGAN ROBSON LEDBURY CRITICS
EDITORIAL & DESIGN	ALICE KATE MULLEN

Poetry Book Society Memberships

Choice

4 Books a Year: 4 Choice books & 4 *Bulletins* (UK £65, Europe £85, ROW £120)

World

8 Books: 4 Choices, 4 Translation books & 4 *Bulletins* (£98, £160, £190)

Complete

24 Books: 4 Choices, 16 Recommendations, 4 Translations & 4 *Bulletins* (£230, £290, £360)

Single copies of the *Bulletin* £9.99

Cover Artwork *Phrase 63* by Safiya Kamaria Kinshasa

ISBN 9781913129422   ISSN 0551-1690

Poetry Book Society | Milburn House | Dean Street | Newcastle upon Tyne | NE1 1LF
0191 230 8100 | enquiries@poetrybooksociety.co.uk

WWW.POETRYBOOKS.CO.UK

LETTER FROM THE PBS

As the nights draw in, it's time to hunker down, draw that extra blanket around you and be transported by some amazing poetry. This Winter's selections will not disappoint!

In their write up for the Translation Choice, Harry Josephine Giles talks of poetry as therapy, "Therapy at its best, though, reminds me very much of poetry: the imposition of form on disordered feeling, the search for rhyme." This seems to sum up much of the work featured in this Winter *Bulletin*, once again helping us readers make sense of the society we are living in, with all its inequality, poverty, desperation and violent past.

I was particularly struck by Choice poet Safiya Kamaria Kinshasa interpreting the voice of her Barbadian ancestors through dance and movement – beautifully explained in her poet piece. I cannot wait to see her perform her poetry and dance – there is a lovely film on our website if you would like a small insight.

I'd like to thank the Ledbury Critics for their insightful work in our review section. And some more farewells; thanks so much to Mona Arshi and Anthony Anaxagorou for their wonderful work as our poet selectors – this is their last round of selections. Jo Clement and Roy McFarlane will take over the task and are busy selecting our Spring titles.

Many of you have taken us up on the T.S. Eliot prize bundle offer – if you have not taken advantage of this amazing deal, it will continue, while stocks last, until the winners' announcements in January 2023.

I'd like to take this opportunity to wish you all a very happy and peaceful Christmas period. As Audre Lorde famously wrote (and the collections in this season's *Bulletin* make clear), "poetry is not a luxury". Please do consider sharing poetry with your friends and family this Christmas – it should not be a luxury, but it does make a GREAT gift!

SOPHIE O'NEILL
PBS & INPRESS DIRECTOR

SAFIYA KAMARIA KINSHASA

Safiya Kamaria Kinshasa is a British born Barbadian raised poet, writer, dancer and choreographer. Her interdisciplinary art braids dance and poetry on the page and stage. Safiya is currently a PhD student in Cultural Studies at the University of Leeds. Safiya is an Obsidian Foundation fellow and an Apples & Snakes/Jerwood Arts Poetry in Performance recipient. In 2022 Safiya was awarded third place in *The London Magazine* Poetry Prize. She is also a national and international spoken word champion. Her work has appeared in a variety of journals including *The Caribbean Writer*, *Poetry Review*, *Poetry London* and *Wasafiri*.

CANE, CORN & GULLY

OUT-SPOKEN PRESS | £11.99 | PBS PRICE £9.00

Cane, Corn and Gully is an electrifying book. This is a debut collection from Safiya Kamaria Kinshasa, a poet who writes with such a naturalness and ease. She interrogates dark and difficult subjects and travels through time and space to Barbados. The quest of the poems is to give voice to the silenced, the forgotten and (often) the vilified, including the Barbadian women that she observes and listens to sensitively. In her hands these acts turn to compassionate poems which take in themes such as violence and historical oppression and hardship. Kinshasa is unafraid to use her tools to wonderful effect.

Her poem 'In Bridgetown, a Man Who Hangs His Socks in a Shopping Trolley Is Saving Up to Buy His Dead Mother a New Hat So She Can Finally Gain Some Control Over The Sun' is a sharp portrayal of a homeless man whom she evokes with tenderness and care. She finishes the poem with these painful but illuminating lines:

> ...Eventually
> we just need to wait for the glass crow to stop
> eating the crumbs passing through his ribs.

Kinshasa is formally adept and playful; she resists being pinned down and there is a dynamic restless quality to the work, an urgency in her lines of verse and a distinct patterning when she employs the Barbadian dialect to give voice to the characters. Kinshasa also arrives at images in surprising ways, but these always feel both natural and arresting, particularly when she ventures into humour and plays with the absurd as a tool to reach something painful she encounters and needs to turn over in the poem:

> A dead coconut did not know it was dead,
> it unbuttoned its blouse and exposed itself

Or in the long sequence 'Choreography: She My Nation':

> A woman in pearls stares at a candle
> who doesn't know he's burning

A fresh and exhilarating read.

MONA ARSHI

SAFIYA KAMARIA KINSHASA

I was brought to my knees reading the colonial reports of enslaved women, but I discovered that if I focused on the descriptions of their movements and dances, I could offer speech from my ancestry which challenged the intolerable stereotypes of Black West-Indian women. Black diasporic dance is an articulation of feeling as well as an entertaining pastime, our gestures are often misinterpreted for wild rants; however, every motif is comprised of a complex intersectional discourse intertwining cultural heritage and emotion. By embodying and narrating the movements of my people, from swinging hips to hands stirring cornmeal, I was able to expand the narratives of rape, torture and oppressive labour sun till sun, to include resilience, hope and joy.

If you crease your face until ravines emerge and shake your fists vigorously in the same manner as a pelican gulping, it is possible you could be communicating vexation, fear, loneliness and intense love. I believe non-verbal communication is often a truer form of expression. This understanding enabled me to return to Barbados with the confidence I could deliver the first poetry collection with labanotation (a graphic score for dance) and the first archive of enslaved women through dance as an interdisciplinary project using poetry.

I danced on the same plantations, gullies and markets where many of the narratives took place to ensure my records were sincere, and with the Barbados Museum and Historical Society I was able to excavate movement with greater understanding. And, during my research I invented a new method to archive Black diasporic dance in a way which encapsulates the non-linear cadence of our dance history, which is constantly evolving. As a neurodiverse writer my work has allowed me to explore poetics in a way which enables me to experience freedom. I see poetry form as choreography, and I am fascinated by decolonising the page and expanding the notion of 'Blackness'.

SAFIYA RECOMMENDS

Robin Coste Lewis, *Voyage of the Sable Venus and Other Poems* (Alfred A. Knopf); Tyehimba Jess, *Olio* (Wave Books); M. NourbeSe Philip, *Zong!* (Silver Press); Ntozake Shange, *For Coloured Girls Who Have Considered Suicide / When the Rainbow Is Enuf* (Simon & Schuster); Joelle Taylor, *C+nto & Othered Poems* (Westbourne Press); Helen Quah, *Dog Woman* (Out-Spoken Press); Keisha Thompson, *Lunar* (Crocus); Fran Lock, *Contains Mild Peril* (Out-Spoken Press); Gboyega Odubanjo, *Aunty Uncle Poems* (Smith/Doorstop Books); Alice Frecknall, *Somewhere Something is Burning* (Out-Spoken Press).

I CHOICE

7

PREFACE: AND IF BY SOME MIRACLE

It was my fifth night terror in a row. I woke in an ocean of sweat and dribble with my thighs burning from running through mahogany trees, cane fields and the bloodcurdling ancestors' screams. Prior to this, I was researching the Trans-Atlantic Slave Trade; although the horrors have never felt less repugnant to read, the void of first-hand narratives from enslaved people (particularly women) was more infuriating than usual, especially now I was reading as a poet. Sometimes I traced texts just to find an utterance, but they were not speaking. And to my devastation, I could not find a single word from an enslaved woman in Barbados. It was my fifth night terror in a row, and I felt myself succumbing to the abyss.

I left the ocean for dry wood, I shook my torso, my fists and stomped my feet. I spread my fingers, stretched my arms to the ceiling, lunged on a diagonal pointing my left toe as far as it could crawl. My hips liaised with the chill from my window, my right knee joined in and a conversation between me and fugitive me began. The discourse lasted for roughly thirty minutes before I realised being able to speak through movement is as much 'inheritance' as it is 'talent'. I immediately browsed through every description I could find of an enslaved person moving (at 2 o'clock in the morning). I discovered the enslaved were speaking, constantly.

CHOREOGRAPHY: SHE MY NATION

Barbados is more ocean dan land
a naturalist tried to write away her soul
her forehead was burned with a new owner's name
i became her when i was forced to let my old coast
fall from my back

breadfruit & bottoms were caught like a fever
past midnight
i tried to undulate my destiny

make note of this

it is now widely accepted dead negroes can move
on their own

followed by de disappointment we don't stay
in we boxes

dis is not a lie   while i here
i confess my parade

i come restoring dawn & liquor
hot like a grown man widdout titty milk
i come de faced de door ah no return

i spit extinction in de eye

you bury my womb in a grave

undestroyed   she   my nation

erased from history for a grapefruit.

SAFIYA KAMARIA KINSHASA

PHILIP GROSS

Philip Gross, born in Cornwall, son of an Estonian wartime refugee, has lived in South Wales since 2004. *The Water Table* (Bloodaxe) won the T.S. Eliot Prize in 2009 and he received a Cholmondeley Award in 2017. He is a keen collaborator, including with artist Valerie Coffin Price on *A Fold in The River* (Seren, 2015), with poet Lesley Saunders on *A Part of the Main* (Mulfran, 2018), with scientists on *Dark Sky Park* (Otter-Barry, 2018) and with the Welsh language poet Cyril Jones in *Troeon/Turnings* (Seren, 2021).

THE THIRTEENTH ANGEL

BLOODAXE BOOKS | £12.00 | PBS PRICE £9.00

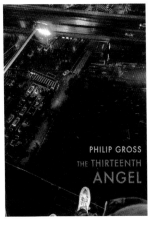

Philip Gross's *The Thirteenth Angel* is a book with its finger firmly on the pulse of the sounds of the contemporary world.

There is a metaphysical vein that runs through all of Gross's work and this book is no exception. This book is more overtly concerned with the sonic properties in the immediacy of the world we inhabit from the "voiceless uvucular fricature" of Arabic to "This smatter on the windscreen, it's the price we pay for speed", no sound is too small or banal to be gathered up in his attention.

Gross uses language which is precise and sharp one moment and then veers into a familiar colloquial style the next which makes him intensely readable. The book is animated by a brilliant first sequence 'Nocturne', which begins:

> Night wired and ticking. Not a wink
> Is not electric: sign to sign, the shut shops
> Half-asleep; street-
> > lights under their hoods;

It's a carefully orchestrated and textured poem, gently gathering in and collecting and naming sounds and relishing language and patterns. The long sinuous form allows Gross to develop and expand his ideas around light and the nature of the spirit.

The Thirteenth Angel stands as the angel of the shadows and in this regard, the angels that inhabit this book stand with us at the edges of perception or disturb the rarest silence.

Gross is an attentive observer with sensitive antennae, and he brings these gifts to the pandemic, a subject which also features in these poems, such as 'Springtime in Pandemia':

> It used to be a dream, the world
> Connected, commonwealth of breath,
> Every border or wall,
> However prickling with watchtowers and surveillance.

MONA ARSHI

PHILIP GROSS

Some poetry collections can look like grand designs, shot through with linking threads of imagery. Reality is usually more interesting than that. The angel's-eye-view tropes had started perching on the ledges of my poems long before I noticed how many they were. From almost-aerial views of London streets in a Britain stumbling towards Brexit, or the autobahns of a Europe struggling to cohere in shock waves of displacement as large as that which sent my refugee father across borders eighty years ago, the sequences pan across landscapes and stretches of time. Each point was a moment's perception. Only afterwards, and at a distance, did I see what they had been mapping – fault lines, lines of stress in bodies politic and in my ageing body too, as the lens I must look through.

Even when the angels become explicit in the changed world of the pandemic, the more directly you look, the more shifting they become. To "believe" in them or not... that isn't the question. Rather, it's what the vision, or illusion, of them reveals about the world. The original word only means "messenger", after all. If there are angels in these poems, they are in, or may actually be, the cracks – not things in themselves but formed by the interfaces between things.

They are alongside, among us, more like Wim Wenders' witnessing angels over Berlin than the unapproachable presences of Rilke's *Elegies*. Near the end of Paul Klee's life, his "taking a line for a walk" produced dozens of hinted-at, emergent angels, wry, unsettling, often very human, and with the approach of war, forbidding. They speak the language of serendipity, of patterns discovered, not planned, that can truly surprise us (as a living poem can and should surprise its writer) though they might just be tricks of the light.

PHILIP RECOMMENDS

Resisting the urge to try to impress with the up-to-the-moment-ness of my reading, here is an honest list of what I've been drawn to, and drawn back to, recently: Gillian Allnutt, *How the Bicycle Shone: New & Selected Poems* (Bloodaxe); John Wedgwood Clarke, *Landfill* (Valley Press); Philippe Jaccottet, *Under Cloudy Skies & Beauregard* (Bloodaxe), trans. Mark Treharne and David Constantine; Jane Monson, *The Chalk Butterfly* (Cinnamon); Denise Riley, *Say Something Back* (Picador); Lesley Saunders, *This Thing of Blood & Love* (Two Rivers).

RECOMMENDATION

Year by year,
look further and the vertigo will deepen

Image: Tom Ritson, Unsplash

THE FOLLIES

Slipping out of the City
in a grey-brown fug,
air full of uncompleted rain.

Behind us, already reduced
to the ghosts of themselves,
the follies of big money:

gherkin, protuberant shapes
of the time. Only the shard
is honest: cloud-capped

splinters. The final push
to the summit... called off
at the snowfield of Forever.

On the way down,
that (statistics tell us)
is when climbers die.

PHILIP GROSS

FRAN LOCK

Fran Lock is the author of numerous chapbooks and ten poetry collections. Her books include *Forever Alive* (Dare-Gale Press, 2022) and *Hyena! Jackal! Dog!* (Pamenar Press, 2021). Fran is the newly appointed Judith E. Wilson Poetry Fellow at Cambridge University. She is an Associate Editor at Culture Matters, a member of the new Editorial Advisory Board for the *Journal of British and Irish Innovative Poetry*, and she edits the Soul Food column for *Communist Review*.

RECOMMENDATION

WHITE/ OTHER

THE87PRESS | £12.99 | PBS PRICE £9.75

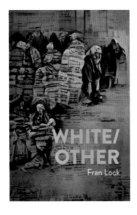

Fran Lock is a poet of exceptional breadth. Her poems, famous for their knotty density, linguistic dexterity and indignation, riff off inequalities and capture in artful detail the sensibilities of those who live on the fringes. In *White/ Other*, Lock's epic meditation on class, poverty and otherness, we see her spin the tricky lyric essay with all the technical prowess of a poet. These are poems at a language level and essays in their search for understanding.

"The time of the poor is wasted time... we do not *require* leisure because we are not capable of *spending* it *profitably*" states Lock in the opening piece 'HORSE FLESH', setting the tone for lyric essays which are as restless and digressive as the worlds they inhabit.

Lock's strength is to effortlessly weave the impolite, the irreverent and the outraged into a hybrid nest of poetry and prose:

> there is a silence in the workshop, when the young woman
> asks me if i'm *sure* i'm white. silence. not embarrassed. but
> expectant

So, begins 'THE WORKSHOP/ THE WITCH', a complex inquiry into otherness through whiteness, the experience of Irish travellers and how they are perceived alongside a robust chronicling of history and persecution.

Elsewhere the book dips into fantasy, an important feature for those who live life in and amongst marginalised people. The ability to imagine an alternative self in a time when so much of that direction is steered by outsiders or onlookers. There is much to unpack in *White/ Other* with the scope of Lock's ambition unable to fit inside such a short summary. If anything, this is more a document, an insight into an upside-down state of affairs.

> feral doesn't want to die but to speak. feral must produce
> strange sounds or no sounds because the mouth is a nest for
> enemy language.

ANTHONY ANAXAGOROU

FRAN LOCK

I wanted a language – a form – for the flex of a muscular fury. I wanted a feral burlesque of queer, working-class rage. I wanted what Jack Halberstam calls "low theory": a model of knowledge eccentrically assembled, refusing to confirm – to conform – to the stale hierarchies of knowing that maintain the status and the functioning of "high theory". Adorno said it: "Even the jokes of those who have been damaged are damaged." Valerie Solanas said it: "Up from the Slime". I didn't want to talk about our anger on anyone else's terms but ours. If "ours" is a punch-drunk republic of two, then I didn't – I don't – especially care.

I wrote *White/ Other* because I needed to understand why somebody I loved very much was no longer alive. I wrote it because for years I had been placing the burden of that "why?" in the wrong place. I wrote it because addiction, depression, and suicidality are perfectly rational responses to a culture and a country that does not want you to exist; when to live at all demands a desperate and impossible strength. I wrote *White/ Other* to get at the way "other" operates through and cancels "white", to articulate an experience of being racialised by poverty and dehumanised by difference, the fatal psychic toll of that, what it does to bodies and minds, what it does at the level of language: the fugitive swerve, the hiccup, the glitch.

I wanted to write through those moments of rupture or realisation – big and small – where the class war became malignantly visible, where I could see both my friend's death and my own grief as enmeshed in its horrible logics. *White/ Other* is my way of writing through to the other side of those logics, the dirty inescapable "normal" of that world by whatever means necessary.

FRAN RECOMMENDS

Carla Harryman, *Cloud Cantata* (Pamenar Press); Safiya Kamaria Kinshasa, *Cane, Corn & Gully* (Out-Spoken Press); Barbara Barnes, *Hound Mouth* (Live Canon); Peter Raynard, *Manland* (Nine Arches Press); Cole Denyer, *CC Death Chartered Institute of Personnel & Development* (Veer). And not new, but never not instructive, inspiring and awesome: Golnoosh Nour, *Rocksong* (Verve) and Claude Cahun, *Disavowals* (Tate).

RECOMMENDATION

Generational poverty:
alternate faces/ identical fates

THE WORKSHOP/ THE WITCH

are you *sure* you're white? and i want to say: as opposed
to what? by which you mean what? law-abiding? educated?
cultured? correct? moral? what accretes around whiteness or
abides within it? by "white" do you really mean "human"
after all? do you mean more or less than skin? a shared fund
of formal tics? those elegant lilting iambics? what belongs to
me. that to which i belong. can carry, can claim. my text is
insurrection, then? or not my text, but the sound of my text
in my mouth, as inseparable from myself? they turn on me. in
a polite and passive-aggressive sort of way. if *they* weren't so
educated, if *they* weren't so cultured, if *they* weren't so moral,
what then? the elite space can't scream "white n****r!" and
they never would, would *they*? the work of their whiteness
is covert, unconscious even, semi-conscious; invisible, refined
and sly. but *they* do say "chav", don't *they*? not to my face,
not usually, but they say it. and they do say "pikey". not
british *or* irish, but both and neither. to look at i am so
white that i disappear daily within the dense crush of *their*
anglophile assumptions. yet i live within those categories as
an alien other: strange, estranged inside of whiteness, because
they don't mean me when they say "white". for them,
"pikey" is a way of removing me from that select community
of whiteness, a form of *lexical* cleansing. "pikey" is also an
eviction, a banishment, a *get thee hence*, a spell of protection.

ARJI MANUELPILLAI

Arji Manuelpillai is a poet, performer and creative facilitator based in London. His poetry has appeared in magazines including *Poetry Wales*, *The Rialto* and *Bath Magg*, and his debut pamphlet *Mutton Rolls* was published by Out-Spoken Press. Arji was shortlisted for the Oxford Prize, the Live Canon Prize, the National Poetry Prize and the Winchester Prize, and was runner-up in the Robert Graves Prize. He is a member of Malika's Poetry Kitchen and London Stanza. He received an Arts Council England award to develop his creative practice and worked with Hannah Lowe as part of the Jerwood Arvon Mentoring Programme.

IMPROVISED EXPLOSIVE DEVICE

PENNED IN THE MARGINS | £9.99 | PBS PRICE £7.50

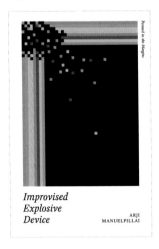

Improvised
Explosive
Device   ARJI
                          MANUELPILLAI

The premise of Arji Manuelpillai's work is to explore, problematise and excavate the way certain social groups are internally formed as a result of disenfranchisement, othering, austerity and desperation. The book invites readers into society's back room. The poem 'Nothing British' opens:

> about
> a sister
>
> tossed from
> a car at 5am
>
> nothing routine
> about spring
>
> appearing all
> over her body

What Manuelpillai builds as the collection progresses is an unsentimental space where those we assume to be dangerous or threatening are living out their lives. One of *Improvised Explosive Device's* great virtues is how it utilises interviews and conversations with several groups ranging from academics to former members of extremist groups such as the EDL, ISIS and the Tamil Tigers.

Interspersed throughout are poems which lean into vulnerability and the family. Masculinity and its various tenets are always in close range, such as the poem 'I Love You Man' which complicates the line between male affection and violence.

A well-networked collection which accommodates areas where overlap and causation meet. For violence to form in an individual's life, it first needs a catalyst, and this is where the book really falls into place. Much of the world is rendered through media sensationalism or misinformation. While Manuelpillai doesn't attempt to exonerate those who've been absorbed into extremist life, he does present readers with an alternative – in other words, the perpetrator at one point was a victim.

This is a set of poems whose intention is to provoke, inspire and alter. At times the humour offers some welcome comic relief while ironically moving the text into a more haunting space.

SELECTOR'S COMMENT

24   ANTHONY ANAXAGOROU

ARJI MANUELPILLAI

Improvised Explosive Device is a project that took three years to write. I was interested in extremism and radicalisation, specifically the question: What are the triggers that push a person to an extreme act of violence. I'm Sri Lankan so found some interesting perspectives from my relatives and family members whose lives were deeply affected by the war in Sri Lanka. But I wanted this book to move away from my life, I wanted it to avoid a focus on one particular group. I wanted the book to be a reflection of the human condition. This proved more challenging than I anticipated. I began to research and reflect on radicalisation in the UK. This included visiting marches and rallies as well as interviewing former EDL and National Front members, current members of other far-right and far-left groups as well as family members who worked with the LTTE. The interviews became the foundations for the book. The act of distilling lived experience into poetry was so interesting to me. I wasn't looking to communicate facts and figures, nor was I looking to create a verbatim response. The poems were trying to capture something else.

The extract below was inspired by a conversation I overheard between two right-wing activists. I was inspired by their love for each other and how that entwined with violence.

> there is always so much violence when we are together
> because there is so much togetherness after the violence.
>
> In the pink of victory, our wounds make eyes in the dark,
> eyes find podiums in our mouths, scars write bios on our bodies;

My view was always that the poems should push the reader to feel something, something so powerful they may themselves understand their own potential for violence and their own personal part to play within this issue.

ARJI RECOMMENDS

When I was researching for *Improvised Explosive Device* I was moved by a whole heap of great books. These included the following: Deborah Landau, *Soft Targets* (Bloodaxe); Mohammed El-Kurd, *Rifqa* (Haymarket Books); Patricia Smith, *Incendiary Art* (Bloodaxe); Tracy K. Smith, *Wade in the Water* (Graywolf); Kaveh Akbar, *Pilgrim Bell* (Vintage); Traci Brimhall, *Come the Slumberless to the Land of Nod* (Copper Canyon); Wayne Holloway Smith, *Love Minus Love* (Bloodaxe).

RECOMMENDATION

you see it now, right there, in the blur, appearing as easy as a story

METHODS OF FITTING IN

The neighbours next door are either having sex or arguing,
I can't tell which, just like I can't decide where to stand
when an anti-racist activist makes monkey noises at the EDL.
I'm on my third draft of a placard and it still feels judgey.
Meet Amrit, soldier at the North Vali torture camp, quiet chap,
tells me nobody knows themselves until they're pushed
to their absolute brink. It doesn't feel much like a placard,
but I imagine myself, hand on valve, edge of a Kalashnikov.
A few years back a black man was on the news talking inflation;
a good friend ripped a slur wide open like a packet of crisps.
I don't mean you though man, you've made an effort to blend in.
I could have been a poorly painted picture politely struck off kilter.
My aunty says: *survival is a matter of keeping a low profile.*

SELINA NWULU

Selina Nwulu is a writer, essayist and social researcher whose work focuses on social and environmental justice, education and global politics. She has toured her poetry extensively, including in Northern India and throughout the UK. Her poetry and essays have been widely published in journals, short films and anthologies including the critically acclaimed anthology *New Daughters of Africa* (Myriad Editions). She was Young People's Laureate for London in 2015 and was shortlisted for the Brunel International African Poetry Prize 2019. Her first pamphlet *The Secrets I Let Slip* was published in 2015 by Burning Eye Books.

RECOMMENDATION

A LITTLE RESURRECTION

BLOOMSBURY | £9.99 | PBS PRICE £7.50

SELINA NWULU

A Little
Resurrection

BLOOMSBURY POETRY

In Selina Nwulu's arresting debut collection *A Little Resurrection* the black female body is charted alongside experiences of place and migration; of language and belonging. The brilliance of Nwulu's project is how she's able to deftly reposition and recast protagonists to highlight the complex and intersectional areas where gender and race overlap to collude and collide.

> Black men with eyes like mine
> frisked and shoved and I wonder whether
> they will resist, or make their limbs and minds
> malleable as bodies coming to the end of breath,
> like the dead waiting to be buried.

From the poem 'Keep the Bodies Buried' which navigates the way race and perception inform each other both locally and internationally.

It would be remiss to think of Nwulu's collection as one solely fixated on the self in relation to a wider more difficult world. It's easy for poets to become engrossed in their lives, their traumas and afflictions. These are poems which look inwards towards the more complex and unsayable, as in the poem 'Unspeakable Things':

> Every session, the physio finds new ways
> to massage unspeakable things
> out of my frame

And yet the book feels finely tuned enough that it manages to pull into its orbit themes and arguments from outside and beyond.

A true highlight of *A Little Resurrection* is its ability to nest itself into the core of its ideas. Be they grief, systemic racism, memory or belonging. The poems, while being well-adjusted to the current political climate, benefit from inhabiting a welcomed vulnerability, a tenderness born out of observation and community, 'Cords That Cannot Be Broken':

> ...One evening
> someone, in jest, starts to sing
>
> *Bind us together, Lord* and without hesitation
> the rest of us rise to our feet, all singing in unison.

ANTHONY ANAXAGOROU

SELECTOR'S COMMENT

SELINA NWULU

> I revisited an old wound, washed it clean
> of my shame and at long last forgave myself.

A Little Resurrection is a collection in search of answers. The poems are trying to find them in unlikely places; in the meal of a man who died too soon to eat it, while sitting with fisherman on a beach in Dakar, Senegal, or in an empty kitchen moments after a robbery.

While themes of blackness, migration and grief, in its many forms, are central to this work, it is ultimately a collection in search of redemption. Whilst writing this, I found myself in need of it, of a faithful anchor to come back to.

And so, my intention is that in and amongst the grief that this book explores, it also shows its longing for something else, more hopeful. Or at least offers a testament to its possibility.

> So we left. Every single one of us
> who'd ever been told to leave the country – gone.
> No one stopped to look at the carcass we left behind
>
> I'd be lying if I said I knew where we all ended up,
> whether this is a happy story.
>
> The month I lived in Dakar
> a shy artist admired the bloom of my skin,
> how much darker I was becoming
> under the sun. A flower finally flourishing.
>
> A year later he told me he missed me
> in English – not his mother tongue –
> so he could be sure I understood
> and the sun shone back on my face.
>
> I'd like to live in that feeling –
> if I could turn it into another country, I would.

SELINA RECOMMENDS

Natalie Diaz, *Postcolonial Love Poem* (Faber); Lucille Clifton, *Good Woman* (Boa Editions); Joshua Bennett, *Owed* (Penguin); Victoria Adukwei Bulley, *Quiet* (Faber & Faber); E.J. Koh, *A Lesser Love* (Pleiades Press); Tiphanie Yanique, *Wife* (Peepal Tree Press); Layli Long Solider, *Whereas* (Picador).

RECOMMENDATION

SAFEKEEPING

My mother has passed on her war,
swallowed stories too dangerous
to leave on her tongue, birthed
them into my core for safekeeping,
the body, Biafra's hiding place.

No wonder I dream of slaughterhouses,
wake up choking, my teeth rimmed
metallic with gunpowder. Why the tips
of my fingers feel haunted.

My mother has passed on her war.
Her memories have run their nails
through my insides. That I might know
I come from a lineage of long prayer
and fears I have no weapons for.

A LITTLE RESURRECTION

There are no last names for the women
who plait your hair early on a Saturday.
The women who know when you say
first thing you mean *first thing* – but still try
and do a quick weave beforehand –
need only be known by their first names.
So, call for Esther, Amina and Barbara,
their voices reverberating off the tired walls
of shops with faded signs. Look for their hot irons
standing to attention, the collection of oils
and creams, and pictures in the window
showcasing an array of hairstyles,
any of which the women will turn their hand to.
Ask them where sells the freshest fish,
who can thread your eyebrows for the best price,
which aunty gives extra maths tuition for the young.
Listen to the cross-examination of local gossip,
cackled anecdotes in four different languages.
Let them orbit the globe of your scalp
as they tug through knots with a wide tooth
and braid the weight of their histories
into your hair, leaving you with a pinched halo
of pain. These women do not care
for last names, but will give you the curve of their hip
to lean on mid-style, will hand over their baby
while they buy more hair for you, before returning
to the sounds of their child babbling on your lap.
Make no mistake, this is neither sentimental nor loving.
This is the unspoken kinship of the not-quite-safe-
on-this-island, those with bodies made so foreign
and ungodly for this country to bear, we do not realise
we are running on half breath until we sit down,
and then see how the women need only offer
the attention of their hands to give us some grace.
Call this a little resurrection, the making of a new crown,
a few hours to look in the mirror and be beautiful.

A.E. STALLINGS

A.E. Stallings is a US born poet and translator who lives in Greece. She studied Classics at the University of Georgia in Athens and Oxford University, and now lives in Athens. She has published four volumes of poetry and three volumes of verse translation, including Lucretius' *The Nature of Things* and Hesiod's *Works and Days* with Penguin Classics. She has been awarded numerous prizes for her translation and poetry, including a Guggenheim fellowship and a MacArthur fellowship. Her poetry book *Like* (FSG) was a finalist for the 2019 Pulitzer Prize.

I SPECIAL COMMENDATION

THIS AFTERLIFE

CARCANET | £15.99 | PBS PRICE £12.00

This book contains highlights from A.E. Stallings's first four books as well as new poems that have never before been collected. The four books are *archaic smile* (1988), *Hapax* (2006), *Olives* (2012) and the Pulitzer nominated *Like* (2018). In many regards this new book is the essential Stallings and reads like an instant classic, as her poems, in a whole variety of forms, are invariably flawless.

The book showcases the great diversity of Stallings's work in poetry. Her early poems demonstrate how the ancient Greek texts (and the ideas contained inside them) inspire and infuse her poems, but her work feels so modern, as she uses the Greek tradition as a lens to talk about everyday life.

Themes that recur in her work include the nature of migration (the brilliant 'Refugee Fugue' is selected here) but also motherhood and the domestic world are subjects too.

> The broken mirror Time will not restore,
> The way your daughter marks you as her own.

Stallings is well known for her use of form, she's hugely skilled in writing in traditional canonical forms including versions of the sonnet and the villanelle, the Ghazal, and the sestina, including the poem 'Like, The Sestina' which playfully interrogates the use of the ubiquitous "filler" word, "like".

> But it's unlikely Like does diddly. Like
> Just twiddles its unopposing thumbs-ups, like-

Her more recent book *Like* has an unusual form of structure (poems are alphabetised) and she experiments more with forms. This is a poet who is very much outward facing and wide awake in the world, as she writes in 'Empathy':

> My love, I'm grateful tonight
> Our listing bed isn't a raft
> Precariously adrift
> As we dodge the coast guard light.

FIRST MIRACLE

Her body like a pomegranate torn
Wide open, somehow bears what must be born,

The irony where a stranger small enough
To bed down in the ox-tongue-polished trough

Erupts into the world and breaks the spell
Of the ancient, numbered hours with his yell.

Now her breasts ache and weep and soak her shirt
Whenever she hears his hunger or his hurt;

She can't change water into wine; instead
She fashions sweet milk out of her own blood.

LAURA DOYLE PÉAN

STUART BELL

Laura Doyle Péan is a communication and cinema graduate, McGill Law and Gender Studies student, poet and activist. As a non-binary Haitian-Quebecois artist, they are interested in the links between language and identity, and in the role art plays in social transformations and social movements. Laura published their first book *Cœur Yoyo* in 2020, and has participated in many artistic productions with the queer feminist collective *Les Allumeuses*.

Stuart Bell is a translator of French literature. He studied Modern Languages at the University of Cambridge where he was later Translator in Residence (2021). His previous publications include *They Stole Our Beauty* (2019), *The Softest Sleep* (2020) and *Bird Me* (2021) which was shortlisted for the 2022 Oxford-Weidenfeld Prize. He also edited the 2021 collection *Moving Impressions: Essays on Art and Experience* and *The South London Cultural Review.*

TRANSLATION CHOICE

YO-YO HEART
TRANSLATED BY STUART BELL

THE87PRESS | £12.99 | PBS PRICE £9.75

LAURA DOYLE PÉAN

Yo-yo Heart

Translated and introduced by Stuart Bell

Halfway through the first day of Laura Doyle Péan's five-day diary, they describe "going to a poetry night / like therapy". I can't find a definite attribution for the dictum that poetry isn't therapy, but whenever I hear it I wonder why it shouldn't be. There's a sense of judgement here: therapy as artless self-indulgence, dull to the outsider, like dreams. Therapy at its best, though, reminds me very much of poetry: the imposition of form on disordered feeling, the search for rhyme.

Doyle Péan's Prologue states clearly that the collection emerges from heartbreak and acute mental distress: a work of learning that "makes beauty out of chaos". In a short week of creation, the speaker of the poems suffers, questions, survives, learns. In what Stuart Bell describes as *poésie dépouillée* ("stripped-back poetry"), they move from where they will "never again / think about tomorrow" to where they can "jump back up".

The poet's tools are as much bitter irony as frank emotion. They paint whole scenes with tremendous economy:

> *cooking soothes* Ricardo tells me
> i cut off the carrot ends
> just like you have
> all contact.

The short lines bear the weight of the joke, the kind of sense-making humour that is common to heartbreak but less often found in poetry. The collection is shaped by a personal map of references to shared pleasures and solitary comforts: Marvel films, the carnival. This specificity gives shape to a story of loss.

At heart, these poems are asking the only questions there are to ask of suffering: Why is this happening and when will it end? Suffering can't answer, because "my suffering is a stranger to me / i am a stranger / to my suffering." By writing through the questions, though, Doyle Péan "can say thank you // to the women who taught me how".

40   HARRY JOSEPHINE GILES

EXTRACTS

i have forgotten how to live
in a flat-share
with myself

sweeping up putting out the bins managing
my own crises
no way of breaking
the lease

...

going to a poetry night
like therapy

my people are a poet
on a cliff edge

depressed
no question about it

for some
the blue sky is enough

mine
has been raining for three days now

MUKAHANG LIMBU

Mukahang Limbu is a three time Foyle Young Poet, winner of the First Story National Competition, and longlisted in the National Poetry Competition. In 2019 he was also the recipient of the Out-Spoken Prize for Poetry. His poems have been published in the anthology *England: Poems from a School* (Picador), *Nascent* (Out-Spoken Press), *The Kindling Journal, Poetry London* and *Tell Me the Truth About Life*, an anthology curated by Cerys Matthews to mark the 25th anniversary of National Poetry Day.

MOTHER OF FLIP-FLOPS

OUT-SPOKEN   PRESS | £8.00 |

The poems in *Mother of Flip-Flops* are languid, playful and gorgeously "sticky with love." Monsoon clouds, moon-gazing, melting mango sorbet – turning each page, I find myself gladly being whisked along in the current of each poem, where luminous details create unexpected sparks of heat inside the lines. Limbu's descriptions vibrate with energy. One small image, from a stand-out poem 'Time Travel to Moon Festival', makes me pause mid-stanza:

> the moss
> of my childhood home
> now blends into
> the black sea of a power-
> cut.

I can almost smell it; I can almost feel its texture, this small patch of moss amidst a darkened city, still and quiet in the centre of a poem in motion as it casts its eye across a dreamscape. There is a sense that the impression might dissolve at any second. The poet invites us to linger "like a shy sound" at the edge of the scene. 'On Cowley Road' begins:

> the sky is an aubergine —
> snow falls from her lilac mouth.

This is an image both familiar and surprising, playful and intimately gorgeous, as the perspective tilts between two snowscapes, one in London and one in the Himalayas. Here Limbu paints another intricate landscape, images accumulating like drifts of snow or like "the clouds across the Himalayas / their blades, / cutting into / sunlight."

These are poems of the body – poems of "monsoon night-song" and mothers and sticky fingers. And maybe the stickiest poem is 'Mango Sorbet', a lush and full-bodied short ode:

> Oh don't we stink of crushed nocturnal insects
> Oh don't we stink of moonlight whipped across our faces

Limbu's poetic voice is versatile and assured, fluidly switching between forms, playing with line length and syntax. This is a brilliant new poet to watch.

ARJI MANUELPILLAI & NINA MINGYA POWLES

I SELECTOR'S COMMENT

MY GRANDFATHER NEVER TOLD US STORIES

about being a father. mother says look
for them in photos of the homecoming Gurkha
with his sons, hair oiled and shirts ironed; shoes neon
clean new — gifts from white man's country — and imagine
how much they cost him. more than

dinner. more than his children's language,
more than the stories he never knew, how his son
ran away from school, how he climbed over gates
in those same western trainers, took the bus
from Kathmandu to his neighbourhood.

my father laughs as he tells us again how he spat
in the air to look for the right way home.

WINTER BOOK REVIEWS

JUANA ADCOCK & JÈSSICA PUJOL DURAN: TEMPORARY ARCHIVES
REVIEWED BY MAGGIE WANG

A formally, tonally, and thematically wide-ranging collection featuring twenty-four women poets from twelve Latin American countries. It is, in the editors' words, a response to the ways in which "the archives of female experience have (been) overlooked". The poems range in subject from honeybees and giving birth to the writing process and mangroves as metaphors for translation. This is a book to return to over and over, to broaden our horizons as readers.

OCT | ARC | £14.99 | PBS PRICE £11.25

TARA BERGIN: SAVAGE TALES
REVIEWED BY DAVE COATES

In a significant formal departure, *Savage Tales* is an expansive series of brief, bleak, witty, psychologically knotted vignettes, akin to Louise Bourgeois' dream journals. What initially feel like aphorisms and comic sketches accumulate into something deeply unsettling, the gradual expression of a fundamental, creeping terror, no less unsettling for its banality: classroom, radio, garden, uninspiring date. *Savage Tales* can be read quickly, but its depth and texture demands close attention.

OCT | CARCANET | £15.99 | PBS PRICE £12.00

CHEN CHEN: YOUR EMERGENCY CONTACT HAS EXPERIENCED AN EMERGENCY
REVIEWED BY OLUWASEUN S. OLAYIWOLA

This book is a wonder, grafting whimsy and seriousness; the elegiac and comic; the self-deprecatory and sublime. Formally interruptive and tonally subversive, here are poems mapping uncanny alternatives inside queerness, sonhood, confession, and the act of writing itself. Chen Chen's eclectic logic is alive, breathing, hungry, and horny, as he proclaims "we can't help but continue to make ourselves." This is restlessness at its finest.

OCT | BLOODAXE | £12.99 | PBS PRICE £9.75

LEDBURY CRITICS TAKEOVER

LINDA FRANCE: STARTLING
REVIEWED BY SHALINI SENGUPTA

It is noteworthy that the first two words of *Startling* are, "it's time". Herein lies the keystone of the collection, held in prismatic contemplation within this suite of poems. France's keen sensitivity to self and landscape, the body and botany, unites the fragmented ruminations of this collection. The poems are capacious and always linguistically interesting; their strengths cumulative, their effects tantalising.

OCT | NWN & FABER | £10.99 | PBS PRICE £8.25

CECILIA KNAPP: PEACH PIG
REVIEWED BY MAGGIE WANG

This debut collection from the Forward Prize shortlisted Young People's Laureate for London, is vivacious, intelligent, and full of surprises. Knapp writes viscerally and candidly on womanhood, the body, family and grief. Her poems are mature yet playful, serious and self-aware, economical but profound. With lines like "I have a memory of your love / like a lodged fishbone", she invites the reader into her utterly unique world and makes us feel at home.

OCT | CORSAIR | £10.99 | PBS PRICE £8.25

ROY McFARLANE: LIVING BY TROUBLED WATERS
REVIEWED BY DAVE COATES

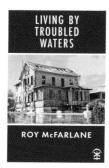

At the core of McFarlane's ambitious third collection is the sequence 'Visitation of the Spirits', an excavation of personal and colonial histories. Its movements from England to the Caribbean, to all corners of the transatlantic, proliferate through the book: McFarlane draws strength and ingenuity from a variety of diasporic traditions. The project is borne aloft by McFarlane's deft, elegant lyric ear, his sweeping, curious and capacious imagination.

OCT | NINE ARCHES PRESS | £10.99 | PBS PRICE £8.25

BOOK REVIEWS

SEAN O'BRIEN: EMBARK
REVIEWED BY SHALINI SENGUPTA

Embark examines the anxiety of language and the inheritance of silence. "The sky is gone," O'Brien writes, "the trees, the birds, the waterfall and we ourselves are stone". These lines build a haunting portrait of annihilation: of bodies hollowed of language and landscapes evacuated of bodies. Yet, even in this expanse of seeming nothingness, his language discloses desire and a repeated invitation to speech. Later poems build an erotics of hold and release, complicating ethical questions of survival and salvage.

NOV | PICADOR | £10.99 | PBS PRICE £8.25

KATIE O'PRAY: APRICOT
REVIEWED BY SHALINI SENGUPTA

Apricot reveals that the most horrific and the most human are both a necessary part of art. The resulting collection is unapologetic in its scope and tender in its pain. Its locus is a body held in a perilous vortex of private longings and public un-belongings: one that has become hardened to the horrors "we spell out / so laboriously with our skeletons". O'Pray revels in the exhilarating possibilities of language, intertwining grief and hope; anger and eroticism; subversion and resistance.

OCT | OUT-SPOKEN PRESS | £11.99 | PBS PRICE £9.00

NEELAM SAREDIA-BRAYLEY: RANI
REVIEWED BY SHALINI SENGUPTA

The opening poems of *Rani* resemble the poet's notebook, gathering together observations and glimmers of thought from many cumulative moments. Later poems interrogate grief and trauma beyond the enclosure of looking and hearing and touching the past. Saredia-Brayley's work represents an urgent reach for the aliveness of memory, language, and attachment. Paying close attention to the aftermath of loss, *Rani* lays claim to life and the relations to come.

OCT | VERVE | £9.99 | PBS PRICE £7.50

YOMI ȘODE: MANORISM
REVIEWED BY OLUWASEUN S. OLAYIWOLA

Șode approaches an array of subjects with fury and candour: contemplations on Black-British masculinity, fatherhood's fragilities and ekphrastic sequences after Caravaggio. Early on, the collection is imbued with a sermonizing tone, though the poems, often narrative and autobiographical, invest in the real-time causes and effects of actions taken and the resulting psychological plights. Vernacular, sacrosanct, and conversational tones cement in this exploration of what it might mean to inherit familial and artistic "manners."

OCT | PENGUIN | £12.99 | PBS PRICE £9.75

DEGNA STONE: PROOF OF LIFE ON EARTH
REVIEWED BY DAVE COATES

Stone's debut is a powerful, vulnerable, often devastating interior odyssey. Though some poems seek the panoramas of Northumbria, or the Tyne's High Level Bridge, the collection largely plays out in a wildly rich inner theatre, in which the real and the teemingly surreal overlap, combine, swap places. The collection asks, with incisive emotional and political analysis, how to survive in a world in which death is a neighbour, in which love and its antithesis go hand in glove.

NOV | NINE ARCHES PRESS | £10.99 | PBS PRICE £8.25

AHREN WARNER: I'M TOTALLY KILLING YOUR VIBES
REVIEWED BY SHALINI SENGUPTA

There is a breathtaking sense of formal ingenuity, irreverent wit, and unapologetic erudition in Warner's lines. As in his previous collections, allusion occupies an almost central position: the poet emerges a bricoleur of sorts as he generates a cross-hatched poetic landscape from disparate sources. Warner traces the performance and dissolution of the self through poems that are both ludic and sincere; manic and darkly comic; subversive and deeply vulnerable.

OCT | BLOODAXE BOOKS | £12.00 | PBS PRICE £9.00

BOOK REVIEWS

WINTER PAMPHLETS

SELIMA HILL: THE HOUSE BY THE SEA

The House By the Sea presents an apocalyptic vision of humanity crushed beneath the weight of "fearless stones / that have outgrown the sea". The beach encroaches upon and entombs the inhabitants of these poems. Merciless, monumental and surreal, the stones admonish us: "they're here to watch, / to coach, / to make us still." This is a chilling reminder of climate catastrophe. Hill's poems weigh heavy upon us, an urgent warning we can no longer ignore.

FAIR ACRE PRESS | £7.50 |

ED. AARON KENT: THE PLUM REVIEW

Poet and publisher extraordinaire Aaron Kent gathers a bumper harvest of plum-based parodies guaranteed to tickle the tastebuds of William Carlos Williams fans. Ranging from the flippant to the political, this book features poems from Ian McMillan to Hollie McNish riffing on the W.C.W. classic. This is just to say... it's a truly tasty anthology and made even more so, because a portion of the proceeds will go to the Trussell Trust to support food banks in the UK.

BROKEN SLEEP BOOKS | £8.99 |

MÍCHEÁL McCANN: KEEPER

In this startling pamphlet, McCann weaves together love poems and elegies, intimate domestic scenes and poems written in the voices of historical figures and characters from television and even video games. McCann has an astonishing way of applying imagery from the natural world to human bodies, not least in the excellent title poem, in which rugby players "run, roll and weave as brave as otters". Exploring, amongst others, themes of masculinity and homosexual love, this is an outstanding read.

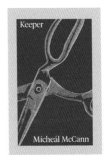

FOURTEEN POEMS | £8.00 |

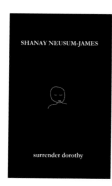

Shanay Neusum-James writes about femininity and black women's bodies through urgent and forceful poems of childhood remembrances, urban scenes, and dark imaginings. The Dorothy poems are among the strongest here, throwing the experience of black girls versus white girls into sharp relief through Neusum-James' memories and reimaginings of her Year 6 school play, in which "she was dorothy and i was black." This is a strong debut which highlights that Neusum-James is definitely one to watch.

BAD BETTY PRESS | £6.00 |

Cracked Asphalt tells a compelling narrative of longing and belonging from Mumbai, India, to Dublin, Ireland. Sree Sen navigates deep nostalgia, "along old Bombay lanes", and the uncertainties of place, race, gender and identity. Whilst one poem claims it's "easier to love in Dublin, here I'm not pretending to be / someone else," the cracks in both "homes" begin to show. A candid sequence which crosses continents and reveals the difficulty of truly feeling at home anywhere.

FLY ON THE WALL | £6.99 |

Milena Williamson's debut pamphlet explores themes of family, history, travel, and politics, with a sensitivity which is moving and effective, particularly in poems such as 'Made in the USA'. Williamson's language is gentle and even musical, as in the line "Feeling grows familiar as I peel a tangerine to smithereens" from the opening poem, 'Stranger'. Fans of Irish poetry will also enjoy spotting the influence of Ciaran Carson and Louis MacNeice upon this work.

GREEN BOTTLE PRESS | £6.00 |

PAMPHLET REVIEWS

WINTER BOOK LISTINGS

PAMPHLETS

Richard Berengarten	The Wine Cup	Shearsman Books	£6.50
Helen Bowie	Exposition Ladies	Fly on the Wall Press	£6.99
Jo Bratten	Climacteric	Fly on the Wall Press	£6.99
Toby Buckley	Milk Snake	The Emma Press	£7.00
John Burnside	Apostasy	Dare-Gale Press	£7.00
Joshua Calladine-Jones	Reconstructions	tall-lighthouse	£8.00
Jonathan Catherall	A Setting In The Flesh	Contraband Books	£10.00
Tom Clucas	The Everyday Unspeakable	Maytree Press	£7.00
Sarah-Clare Conlon	cache-cache	Contraband Books	£10.00
Stewart Conn	Underwood	Mariscat Press	£7.50
Michaela Coplen	Finishing School	ignitionpress	£6.00
Adriana Díaz Enciso	Flint	Contraband Books	£10.00
Iulia David	Blueprint	Green Bottle Press	£6.00
Will Eaves	Exposed Staircase	Rack Press	£5.00
Taylor Edmonds	Back Teeth	Broken Sleep Books	£6.99
Kate Frances	Daydream Erratica	Broken Sleep Books	£6.99
Remi Graves	with your chest	fourteen publishing	£8.00
Eve Grubin	Grief Dialogue	Rack Press	£5.00
Ella Sadie Guthrie	Poems for Pete Davidson	Broken Sleep Books	£6.99
Cleo Henry	The Last Lesbian Bar in the Midlands	fourteen publishing	£8.00
Selima Hill	Men in Shorts	Fair Acre Press	£7.50
Selima Hill	The House By The Sea	Fair Acre Press	£7.50
Lucy Holme	Temporary Stasis	Broken Sleep Books	£6.99
Alun Hughes	Down the Heavens	Yew Tree Press	£5.00
Christopher James	The Storm in the Piano	Maytree Press	£7.00
Aaron Kent	The Plum Review	Broken Sleep Books	£8.99
Robert Kiely	ROB	Broken Sleep Books	£6.99
Dal Kular	(un)interrupted tongues	Fly on the Wall Press	£6.99
Lauren Lawler	Physical Education	Green Bottle Press	£6.00
Mukahang Limbu	Mother of Flip-Flops	Out-Spoken Press	£8.00
Hannah Linden	The Beautiful Open Sky	V. Press	£6.50
Fran Lock	Forever Alive	Dare-Gale Press	£7.99
Mícheál McCann	Keeper	fourteen publishing	£8.00
James McDermott	Green Apple Red	Broken Sleep Books	£6.50
Hilary Menos	Fear of Forks	HappenStance Press	£6.00
David Nash	The Islands of Chile	fourteen publishing	£8.00
Shanay Neusum-James	surrender dorothy	Bad Betty Press	£6.00
Emily Oldfield	Calder	Poetry Salzburg	£7.00
Gita Ralleigh	Siren	Broken Sleep Books	£6.99
Jacob Anthony Ramírez	Kitchen Boombox	ignitionpress	£6.00
Andreea Iulia Scridon	Calendars	Broken Sleep Books	£6.99
Sree Sen	Cracked Asphalt	Fly on the Wall Press	£6.99
Richard Skinner	Dream into Play	Poetry Salzburg	£7.50
Michael Vince	A Conversation with George Seferis	Rack Press	£5.00
Ray Vincent-Mills	Creature Without Building	V. Press	£6.50
Milena Williamson	Charm for Catching a Train	Green Bottle Press	£6.00

TRANSLATIONS

Laura Doyle Péan, trans. Stuart Bell	Yo-Yo Heart	the87press	£12.99
Philippe Jaccottet, trans. Tim Dooley	In Winter Light	Two Rivers Press	£12.00
Aleš Šteger, trans. Brian Henry	Burning Tongues	Bloodaxe Books	£14.99
Marina Tsvetaeva, trans. Christopher Whyte	Head on a Gleaming Plate	Shearsman Books	£12.95

FEATURING

Laura Doyle Péan | Philip Gross | Safiya Kamaria Kinshasa
Mukahang Limbu | Fran Lock | Arji Manuelpillai | Selina Nwulu | A.E. Stallings

£9.99

ISBN 978-1-913129-42-2

9 781913 129422 >